A *Marriage Preparation Supplement* designed to
help couples understand and embrace...

GOD'S PLAN FOR A JOY-FILLED

Marriage

Instructor's Edition

based on John *Paul II's Theology of the Body*
and the book *Good News About Sex & Marriage*

By Christopher West

Abbreviations

CCL *Code of Canon Law* (Canon Law Society of America, 1983)

CCC *Catechism of the Catholic Church,* Second Edition (Libreria Editrice Vaticana, 1997)

FC *Familiaris Consortio,* John Paul II's Apostolic Exhortation on the Christian Family (Pauline, 1981)

GN *Good News About Sex and Marriage, Revised Edition,* Christopher West (St. Anthony Messenger Press, 2004)

KW *Karol Wojtyla: The Thought of the Man Who Became John Paul II,* Rocco Buttiglione (Eerdman's, 1997)

LF *Letter to Families,* John Paul II's Letter in the Year of the Family (Pauline, 1994)

LR *Love & Responsibility,* Karol Wojtyla's (John Paul II's) philosophical work on sexuality (Ignatius Press, 1993)

RH *Redemptor Hominis,* John Paul II's Encyclical Letter on the Redeemer of Man (Pauline, 1979)

TB *The Theology of the Body, John Paul II's Addresses on Human Love in the Divine Plan* (Pauline 1997)*

VS *Veritatis Splendor,* John Paul II's Encyclical Letter on the Splendor of Truth (Pauline, 1993)

*For ease of reference, page numbers provided refer to this edition. However, please note that the 1997 one-volume edition of the Pope's catechesis was copyedited and may differ slightly from the original Vatican translation quoted in this workbook.

Nihil obstat:	Mr. David Walker Censor Deputatus
Imprimatur:	+Most Rev. Charles J. Chaput, O.F.M. Cap. Archbishop of Denver June 1, 2005

Cover Design: Devin Shadt

Printed in the United States of America

ISBN 13: 978-1-932927-42-9

Table of Contents

Instructor's Introduction

Background Information

Helping prepare engaged couples to embrace God's plan for the Sacrament of Marriage is an honor and a privilege. In today's climate, it is also a challenge. *God's Plan for a Joy-Filled Marriage* is a marriage preparation course designed specifically to help meet that challenge.

The content, approach, and flow of this course were developed, tested, and refined over several years based on the experience of instructing approximately 2000 engaged couples in Catholic teaching. It will continue to remain a work in progress as on-going experience suggests ever-better ways to present the material. Still, it has proven very successful in helping couples understand and embrace "God's plan for a joy-filled marriage."

When this *Instructor's Edition* (IE) is open and lying flat, you will notice that instructor information such as logistics, notes, and suggestions for your presentation appear on the left page while course content appears on the right page. The course content (except for the answers in red) is exactly the same as the couple's edition (CE). The page numbers for course content are the same in both the IE and the CE for ease of reference while teaching the class. While the course content is clearly and logically set forth in the workbook, rote regurgitation of information will do little to inspire the couples who take this class. Thus, you are strongly encouraged to "take ownership" of the course through your own personal presentation style, stories and examples from your own life, favored analogies, anecdotes, etc.

A Note on the Accompanying Text

Today a great deal of confusion exists, even among clergy and trained catechists, regarding the specifics of Catholic teaching on marriage and sexuality. The accompanying text *Good News About Sex & Marriage* was written specifically to explain and clarify not only the *whats*, but also the *whys* of Catholic teaching about sex and marriage. Written with today's engaged couples in mind, it provides answers to all the "tough" questions you can expect to be asked and need to be prepared to answer. In short, thorough knowledge of the contents of *Good News...* is a *must* for teaching the class (note that the workbook references specific page numbers in the margin for further information on corresponding topics).

Faith should be *Proposed,* Not *Imposed*

A wide gulf often exists between the Church's teaching and the attitudes, beliefs, and behavior of today's engaged couples. In upholding the Church's teaching, we must be careful never to project an air of indignation or self-righteousness. Without compromising the radical demands of marital love, we are to invite, exhort, challenge, proclaim, and propose with patience and with love — but never condemn.

God's Plan for a Joy-Filled Marraige works from the premise that Catholic teaching can never be *imposed,* only *proposed,* especially in our modern culture where messages that are contrary to the

Catholic vision of marital love are commonplace. We realize that we are presenting the Church's vision to a skeptical audience that will ask many valid and understandable questions. We also know that pastoral sensitivity is vital to transmitting the message successfully.

We believe that when Catholic teaching is upheld in its full splendor, it does not need to be foisted on anyone. Men and women are naturally attracted to the beauty of God's plan for marital love; most couples simply have never heard it presented in a sensible, appealing way. *God's Plan for a Joy-Filled Marriage* seeks to do just that — to present the fullness of Catholic teaching on marital love in all its beauty; the rest is in God's hands.

The Audience

It's also very important for instructors to have a clear understanding of the cultural situation in which today's engaged couples have been raised. If contemporary couples are to receive the Church's teaching on marriage and sexuality as the *good news* that it is, we must proclaim it in a way that demonstrates an understanding of their values, challenges, hopes, fears, mind-sets, and language. We must be ready and willing to employ new methods and approaches in our teaching that convincingly demonstrate how the Church's vision of marriage and sexuality perfectly corresponds to the deepest desires of the human heart for love and personal union.

The following information is provided to help you better understand the audience you'll be addressing.[1]

The Cultural Situation

The American cultural landscape provides both bright spots and shadows for today's couples preparing for marriage. On the one hand, couples coming to the Church today for marriage have been raised in a culture that instills in them greater attention to the quality of their interpersonal relationship and a keen awareness of their equal dignity as men and women. On the other hand, many couples have grown up without the stable witness of their own parents' married love.

Furthermore, American culture loudly and incessantly promotes a vision of human life that is not only unsupportive of marriage and family life, but quite often antithetical to them. While some might feel pessimistic in the face of current trends, as Christians, we have great confidence and hope. We are convinced that we have *good news* to share with the engaged and that the Holy Spirit can work powerfully to transform lives through our humble and imperfect efforts. By proclaiming the full truth of conjugal love to engaged couples, and by directing them to full participation in the sacramental life of the Church, we lay the building blocks of a "culture of life."

Profile of Couples Seeking Marriage in the Church

While it's important to avoid unfounded prejudices with regard to specific couples, it's just as important to have a realistic understanding of the general circumstances in which many couples today are approaching the Church to receive the Sacrament of Marriage.

Some of the common issues/circumstances with which couples are dealing and which call for specific pastoral concern include the following:

- lack of initial conversion to Christ and his Church
- weak or non-existent faith
- uncatechized Catholics
- inactive Catholics
- mixed faith
- new-age spirituality
- individualism and materialism
- deficient understanding of the nature of marriage
- cohabitation/current sexual activity
- contraceptive practice and mentality
- previous sexual relationships
- couples generally older than in the past
- dual careers
- children of divorced parents
- divorce mentality
- second union
- seeking validation of civil union
- abusive backgrounds (child abuse, molestation, abusive dating relationships, rape)
- abusive relationship (verbal, emotional, and physical abuse)
- personal or parental alcohol or drug abuse or addiction
- previous abortion
- sexual addiction (extended involvement with pornography and masturbation, repeated sexual encounters, anonymous sexual encounters, repeated infidelity in mind and/or action, etc.)

The Primary Goal of this Class

Divorce rates of those who marry in the Catholic Church are not significantly different from the rest of society. This is connected to the fact that Catholics are entering marriage with many of the same detrimental patterns of thinking and behaving as the general population, such as those characteristic of the list above.

This is the bad news. The good news is that the Catholic Church has the "blueprint" for successful marriages. She teaches that if marriages are to succeed two things are necessary: first, couples must meditate upon God's plan for marriage; and second, they must seek to shape all their ways of thinking and acting according to it.[2] *Helping the engaged to do these two essential things is the primary goal of this class.*

The high rates of divorce among Catholics indicate that this task has not always been carried out successfully. Loss of faith in the Church's role as the authentic interpreter of God's plan for marriage is partly to blame for this. Also, many couples come to the Church for marriage without an explicit personal attachment to Jesus Christ.

Thus, above all else, instructors of this class must consider themselves evangelists. With clear respect for the freedom of each person, we must encourage an encounter with the risen Christ through a call to faith in the truths of Catholicism. John Paul II encouraged the Church in America to "speak increasingly of Jesus Christ, the human face of God and the divine face of man. It is this proclamation that truly makes an impact on people, awakens and transforms hearts, in a word, converts. Christ must be proclaimed with joy and conviction, but above all by the witness of each one's life."[3]

This class has been designed in light of John Paul II's call for "a serious preparation of young people for marriage, one which clearly presents Catholic teaching on this sacrament at the theological, anthropological, and spiritual levels."[4] Such preparation is an integral part of the "new evangelization" of which the church so often speaks.

Pastoral experience attests that those who are properly evangelized and catechized, that is, those who have encountered Christ personally and who understand, embrace, and strive to live the fullness of the Church's teaching on marriage, very rarely divorce. Of course, a one-day class can only introduce couples to the Church's teaching. Still, we can be assured that when the truth is lovingly proclaimed, it does not return empty. As we remain faithful to Christ and his Bride, our work will bear fruit in the lives of those we instruct.

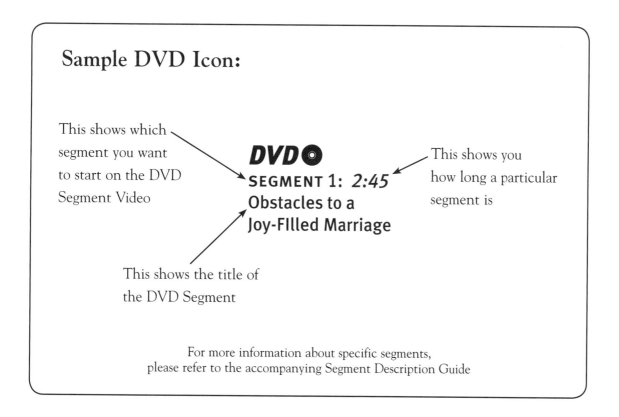

Sample DVD Icon:

This shows which segment you want to start on the DVD Segment Video

DVD ◉
SEGMENT 1: *2:45*
Obstacles to a Joy-FIlled Marriage

This shows you how long a particular segment is

This shows the title of the DVD Segment

For more information about specific segments, please refer to the accompanying Segment Description Guide

---

[1]This information is adapted (with permission) from *What God Has Joined: Supplement to the Particular Norms for Christian Marriage in the Archdiocese of Denver* (Dec 31, 2000).

[2]*See Pius XI, Casti Connubii, n. 2.*

[3]*John Paul II, The Church in America, n. 67*

[4]*Ibid, n. 46*

"True love" is possible. That's the promise the church holds out to us in her teachings on sex and marriage. This is good news. This is great news!

GN, p. 18

Purpose of this introductory talk:

- to put couples at ease and make them feel welcome;
- to preview the schedule;
- to provide an overview of what the class will (and will not) cover;
- to familiarize couples with the workbook and its relation to the text book.

Logistics: Class should begin with an appropriate prayer, followed by introductions. First help the couples get to know you by sharing a bit about your own life, your own marriage (if you're married), and why you enjoy working with engaged couples. Then ask each couple to stand and introduce themselves. Have them give their names, when they're getting married, and possibly a short story about how they met.

After the introductions, have them follow along in their workbooks as you introduce the class. Personal introductions and the following intro to the class should take approximately 30 minutes.

Suggestion: Explain why it not only makes sense, but why it is essential to turn to God to understand marriage. Marriage is not a human idea. It is created by God and subject to his laws, etc..

Introduction

1. The Key to a Joy-Filled Marriage

In 1930, the Pope at the time (Pius XI) wrote a letter on Christian Marriage. His goal was to respond to some trends in thought that devalued marriage and equip couples to experience a joy-filled life together. In his opening paragraphs, he stated that if couples are to know true joy in their married life, two things are necessary:

- First, couples must meditate upon God's plan for married life.

- Second, with the help of God's grace, couples must shape all their ways of thinking and acting according to God's plan.

This is the two-fold goal of this marriage preparation course: to present a summary of Catholic teaching on God's plan for marriage, and to offer practical suggestions for embracing it in your own lives.

DVD
SEGMENT 1: *2:45*
Obstacles to a
Joy-Filled Marriage

121-124 *DVD*
SEGMENT 2: *4:45*
Laying the Foundation
for the Program

17-30
45-64

2. Important Points to Keep in Mind

We extend a special welcome to all non-Catholics.

- We recognize that non-Catholics may have some reservations about attending a Catholic marriage prep program and we want to put you at ease.

- We are confident that this class will not only help you understand your future spouse's faith, but will also benefit you. The word "Catholic" means universal. We believe anyone who thoughtfully engages Catholic teaching on marriage and sexuality can benefit. We hope you will agree.

Catholic teaching can never be *imposed*, only *proposed*.

- Without hiding our hope that each of you will come to embrace the richness of God's plan for marriage, this class is not intended to "force" anything upon you, only to propose an authentic Catholic vision of God's plan for marriage.

DVD
SEGMENT 3: *4:00*
Guiding Principles
of the Program

37-38

Note: This point is particularly important. Many couples come to marriage preparation classes with expectations of learning communication skills, how to handle conflict, etc. It's important to clarify up-front what this class is and is not about. Help the couples understand that this class is only one step in the overall process of marriage preparation.

Note: Unless otherwise noted, Points to Ponder are intended for each couple's further reflection outside of class.

- Accepting or rejecting the proposal is – and must always be – entirely up to you. We only ask that you keep an open mind and consider whether the vision of marital love presented here corresponds with the deepest desires of your heart.

This is not an all-encompassing marriage prep program, but only one important step in a larger process.

- Communication skills, handling conflict, finances, decision making, parenting – all of these and many other topics are important with regard to preparing for marriage, but they will not be addressed in this class.

- As the title indicates, the specific goal of this class is to help you understand *God's plan* for a joy-filled marriage. We encourage you to work closely with your preparing priest or deacon to fulfill other steps in the overall process of marriage preparation.

3. About this Workbook & the Accompanying Text

DVD
SEGMENT 4: *5:15*
Overview of
the Program

The course consists of six main presentations and four private reflection exercises. This workbook will serve both as your guide through the course and as a resource for further reflection.

- The blank spaces allow for audience participation during the course. An answer key is provided in the back (but don't look ahead!).

- Numbers in the margins refer to pages for further study on given points in the accompanying text, *Good News About Sex & Marriage* (revised edition; if you have the original edition some pages may not be correct).

- Shaded areas called *"Points to Ponder"* are provided to encourage further personal and couple reflection.

- Each section of the notes concludes with a three-point summary.

While this class provides a good overview of Catholic teaching, you're bound to leave with questions. The accompanying text, *Good News About Sex & Marriage*, addresses 115 of the most common questions and objections that today's couples have about Catholic teaching. We strongly recommend that you take time before your wedding to read and discuss *Good News* together as a couple.

Part I:

Catholic *Faith* & Your Marriage

Purpose of this talk:

- to provide an overview of God's original plan for marriage as described in the Book of Genesis;
- to help couples understand the effects of original sin on man and woman's relationship;
- to help couples understand the effects of original sin in their own relationship;
- to help couples understand their need for redemption in Christ.

Logistics: Explain the "fill-in-the-blank" approach as a technique to facilitate learning. This talk should last approximately 40 minutes.

Throughout the Old Testament, God's love for his people is described as the love of a husband for his bride. In the New Testament, Christ *embodies* this love.

GN, pp. 18-19

God's Plan for Marriage "In the Beginning":

Male & Female He Created Them

1. The Bible & Marriage

We might not think the Bible has much to say about marriage. Yet, in a certain sense, the Bible from beginning to end is a story about (1) _____marriage_____.

18

- The Bible begins and ends with marriages — Adam-Eve and Christ-Church.

- We can look to these marital "book ends" of Genesis and Revelation as a key for interpreting what lies between.

- Applying this analogy we learn that God's eternal plan is to "marry" us (see Hos 2:19).

19

- God wanted this eternal "marital plan" to be so obvious to us that he stamped an image of it in our very being by creating us as male and female and calling us to marriage.

"'For this reason a man shall leave his father and mother and be joined to his wife, and the two shall become one flesh.' This is a great mystery, and I mean in reference to Christ and the church" (Eph 5:21-32).

21

- In this way marriage becomes a "sacrament" or physical sign of God's love in the world.

- The human body and sex, then, are not only biological realities, but theological realities.*

1a. "The Church cannot therefore be understood …unless we keep in mind the 'great mystery' involved in the creation of man as male and female and the vocation of both to conjugal love, to fatherhood and to motherhood" (LF, n. 19).

18

* This workshop is based largely on a collection of 129 short talks by Pope John Paul II known as the Theology of the Body. The beautiful vision of the human body, marital love, and sexual union outlined in these talks has already begun a sexual "counter-revolution." To learn more, visit TheologyOfTheBody.com

Note: It's important to stress, with the help of this quote, the nature of marriage and sexual love as an analogy of God's love. God is not sexual. Nor is Christ's love for the Church "sexual," as we typically understand that term. Without these important clarifications there remains the possibility of serious misunderstanding. God's love and mystery always remain far beyond any human image or concept.

Suggestion: See the "flat tire" analogy on the video as an example of how to explain the importance of Christ's words here.

Suggestion: Since many people believe science has made the creation stories of Genesis irrelevant, it's important to address objections up-front. See the "optometrist" example on the video.

Suggestion: The fact that God refers to himself in the plural (Let us...) provides an opportunity to clarify our belief in the Trinity. Clarity of thinking about this most fundamental doctrine (one God in three Persons, that Jesus as Son of God is truly divine, etc.) shouldn't be assumed.

1b. "It is obvious that the analogy of earthly ...spousal love cannot provide an adequate and complete understanding of ...the divine mystery." God's "mystery remains transcendent in regard to this analogy as in regard to any other analogy, whereby we seek to express it in human language" (TB, 330).

2. Christ Provides the Key to a Joy-Filled Marriage

DVD⊙
SEGMENT 3: *3:30*
Jesus and Our
Hardness of Heart

"For your hardness of heart Moses allowed you to divorce your wives, but from the beginning it was not so" (Mt 19:8).

22-25

- Jesus is trying to help us realize that something deep in the human heart has disturbed God's original plan for marriage.

- What was it? If we answer this question we will discover the root cause of all marital problems ...*and* pave the way for a solution to those problems.

2a. "According to faith the disorder we notice so painfully [in the male-female relationship] does not stem from the nature of man and woman, nor from the nature of their relations, but from sin. As a break with God, the first sin had for its consequence the rupture of the original communion between man and woman" (CCC, n. 1607).

2b. "Jesus came to restore creation to the purity of its origins" (CCC, n. 2336).

2c. The first man and the first woman must serve as the model for all men and women who enter marriage and unite in "one flesh" (see TB, 50).

3. Created in God's Image

DVD⊙
SEGMENT 4: *7:00*
Imaging God
through Our Love

"Then God said: 'Let us make man in our image, after our likeness.' ...God created man in his own image; ...male and female he created them. And God blessed them and God said to them 'Be fruitful and multiply'" (Gen 1:26-27).

19-20

- This means that somehow, in the complementarity of the sexes, we *image* God. Somehow, as male and female, we make *visible* God's *invisible* mystery.

- What is God's invisible mystery?

3a. "God has revealed his innermost secret: God himself is an eternal exchange of love, Father, Son, and Holy Spirit, and he has destined us to share in that exchange" (CCC, n. 221).

Suggestion: This is an excellent opportunity to comment on the link in all of our hearts to the Church's teaching. We are all looking for love — we know this to be true in our hearts. We also know our happiness depends on finding real love. Sadly, we are so starved for love, we are often willing to "eat out of a dumpster" to satisfy that hunger. Everything the Church teaches about sex and marriage serves this essential purpose: to help us distinguish between authentic love and its counterfeits.

Suggestion: It is helpful to give examples of these qualities of God's love. For instance: God didn't need to create us (free); Christ gives himself completely to us on the cross (total); God will never forsake us (faithful); and Christ came so that we might have life to the full (fruitful).

Suggestion: This is a great opportunity to dispel the notion that the Church is "down on sex." Sex, in the eyes of the Church, is more beautiful and glorious than we could ever imagine. The problem with our culture is not that it over-values sex. Quite the contrary, our culture has no idea how valuable sex is!

3b. "Creating the human race in his own image, ...God inscribed in the humanity of man and woman the vocation ...of love and communion" (FC, n. 11).

3c. "Man cannot live without love. He remains a being that is incomprehensible for himself, his life is senseless, if love is not revealed to him, if he does not ...experience it and make it his own" (RH, n. 10).

3d. The human person images God "not only through his own humanity, but also through the communion of persons which man and woman form right from the beginning.... On all this, right from the beginning, there descended the blessing of fertility" (TB, 46).

4. Loving as God Loves

19-20

DVD●
SEGMENT 5: *3:30*
The Four Characteristics
of Marital Love

"This is my commandment, that you love one another as I have loved you" (Jn 15:12). "Therefore a man leaves his father and his mother and cleaves to his wife, and they become one flesh" (Gen 2:24).

- There are numerous ways to describe God's love, but four qualities in particular stand out. God's love is (2) _____free_____, _____total_____, _____faithful_____, and _____fruitful_____.

- Another name for this kind of love is (3) _____marriage_____.

- This is precisely what bride and groom commit to at the altar and express with their whole selves (body and soul) by becoming "one flesh."

- God designed sexual intercourse so we could mirror his own eternal, life-giving love!

4a. "Every man and every woman fully realizes himself or herself through the sincere gift of self. For spouses, the moment of conjugal union constitutes a very particular expression of this. It is then that a man and a woman [are meant to] become a mutual gift to each other" (LF, n. 12).

 POINTS TO PONDER

Is marriage the only vocation that reflects our creation as male and female in the image of God? If not, what other vocation(s) correspond to our call to love as God loves?

163-171

5. Nakedness Revealed God's Original Plan of Love

DVD●
SEGMENT 6: *5:00*
Naked without Shame

"And the man and his wife were both naked, and were not ashamed" (Gen 2:25).

Suggestion: The important point to emphasize here is that Christ's commandment to "love as he loves" is stamped right in our bodies, right in our sexuality. In other words, the call to marriage is revealed precisely by sexual difference. This is also a great opportunity to dispel the notion that the Church is "down on sex." According to John Paul II, if we live according to the truth of our sexuality we fulfill the very meaning of life (which is to love as God loves). But the opposite is also true. If we don't live according to the truth of our sexuality, we compromise the meaning of our existence and forfeit true happiness.

Suggestion: This is an excellent opportunity to dispel a common myth about Christian belief, namely, that the 'spirit is good' and the 'body is bad.' Holiness expressed through the body is an expression of the entire person: body, mind and spirit. Often our tendency is to think our spiritual lives in some disembodied way. However, the theology of the body is restating the Christian belief that our bodies were created for holiness and it is in and through our bodies that we offer the expression of our mind and spirit. It is through our bodies that our "whole" person offers a sincere gift of himself. This concept should be shared with the engaged couples.

Suggestion: As this Point to Ponder suggests, it's helpful to appeal to the way men and women experience sexual desire and contrast that with God's original plan. For example, when a woman in a bikini is trying to sell beer on a billboard, do men react with the desire to make a total gift of themselves in the image of God? Why not? This provides a helpful segue into the discussion of original sin.

Important Note: In the videos, Christopher uses the phrase "God is pro-choice" to illustrate a very important point—that God gives us the gift of free will, which is the capacity to choose between good and evil. He also uses this phrase in an attempt to reclaim a terribly abused word— "choice"—which has been co-opted to justify the greatest evil in our culture today—abortion. Christopher's use of the term "pro-choice" is in no way intended to imply that God is for the right to choose abortion. The words of Scripture and the constant teaching of the Church clearly show that God wants us to value life, regardless of the cost to us. Speaking of the invaluable gift of life, God says, "I have set before you life and death, blessing and curse; therefore choose life, that you and your descendants may live" (Deuteronomy 30:19; RSV).

- Pope John Paul II calls this the "key" for understanding God's original plan for man and woman (see TB, 52).

- They experienced sexual desire only as the desire to love in God's image. There was no shame (or fear) in love. "Perfect love casts out fear" (1 Jn 4:18).

5a. Nakedness reveals the **nuptial meaning of the body** which is the body's "capacity of expressing love: that love precisely in which the person becomes a gift and — by means of this gift — fulfills the very meaning of his being and existence" (TB, 63).

5b. "'Nakedness' signifies the original good of God's vision" (TB, 57). "God saw everything that he had made, and behold, it was very good" (Gen 1:31).

5c. Their nakedness demonstrates that "holiness entered the visible world." It is "in his body as male or female [that] man feels he is a subject of holiness." Holiness is what "enables man to express himself deeply with his own body... precisely by means of the 'sincere gift' of himself" (TB, 76-77).

 POINTS TO PONDER

If this is the way God created sexual desire, why isn't this the way we experience it?

6. God Gave Us the Capacity to Choose (But Some Choices Are Always Wrong)

23-26

DVD⬤
SEGMENT 7: *5:00*
The Effect of Original Sin and the Gift of Free Will

"And the Lord God commanded the man saying, 'You may freely eat of every tree of the garden; but of the tree of the knowledge of good and evil you shall not eat, for in the day that you eat of it, you shall die'" (Gen 2: 16-17).

- Why was this commandment only given to "Adam" and not the animals? The human person is the only creature in the visible world with (4) _____freedom_____. This is why "there was not found a helper fit for him" (Gen 2:20) among the animals.

- Freedom is given as the capacity to (5) _____love_____, to do good and avoid evil. But how do we know what is good and what is evil? How do we know what is loving and what is not?

- As his *creatures*, we must trust in God's providence and not seek to determine good and evil for ourselves. The moment we do, we cut ourselves off from the life and happiness God intends. We "die."

Suggestion: Remind the couples once again that the goal here is to try to get to the root of all marital problems and difficulties. That root is what Christians call "sin." It is a basic "self-focus" rather than a focus on God and others. It stems from a deep sense of distrust of God and others. This story uses symbolic language to help us understand why we have this rebellion in our hearts towards God. Only if we overcome this distrust and place faith in God and his plan for marriage will we ever experience the joy and happiness we're looking for.

6a. *The "power to decide what is good and what is evil does not belong to man, but to God alone." Man "possesses an extremely far reaching freedom, since he can eat 'of every tree of the garden.' But his freedom is not unlimited: it must halt before the 'tree of the knowledge of good and evil,' for it is called to accept the moral law given by God" (VS, n. 35).*

6b. *"The 'tree of the knowledge of good and evil' symbolically evokes the insurmountable limits that man, being a creature, must freely recognize and respect with trust. Man is dependent on his Creator and subject to ...the moral norms that govern the use of freedom" (CCC, n. 396).*

7. A Snake in the Marital Garden
25

The Serpent said to the woman, "Did God say, 'You shall not eat of any tree in the garden'? ...You will not die. For God knows that when you eat of it your eyes will be opened, and you will be like God, knowing good and evil" (Gen 3:1-5).

- The implication: God doesn't want you to be like him; God is withholding something from you; God doesn't (6) _____love_____ you. His commands aren't for your happiness. If you really want to be happy, don't listen to God. Do your own thing.

- Because of this insidious deception, men and women throughout history have bought into the lie that God is not our loving Father, but our enemy.

- There has been a constant pressure on us to reject God, even to the point of hating him. Following his will comes to be seen not as the sure road to happiness that it is, but as a threat to our happiness.

8. The Entrance of Shame
25-26

"Then the eyes of both were opened, and they knew that they were naked; and they sewed fig leaves together and made themselves aprons" (Gen 3:7).

- When they disobeyed God, what "died" was the love of God in their hearts. Void of God's inspiration, sexual desire became inverted, self-seeking.

- Lust, therefore, is sexual desire void of God's love. It is a "reduction" of God's original plan. It doesn't offer more, but less.

Suggestion: Close by reminding the couples that recognizing lust, selfishness, and sin in our lives and in our relationships should not be cause for despair — welcome to the human race! Instead, it should spur us on to accept with great joy the "good news": there is a solution. This is why the story about Jesus Christ is called the "Gospel," the "good news." Christ came into the world to restore the original plan of love deep in men and women's hearts. If we open to that gift and live in it every day, we have the necessary means for overcoming our difficulties day-by-day and living a joy-filled marriage.

• We cover our bodies in a fallen world not because they are bad, but because they are "very good" and we want to protect their goodness from the degradation of lust.

DVD●
SEGMENT 8: *6:30*
The Entrance of Shame
and the Battle Between
Love and Lust

8a. "Man is ashamed of his body because of lust. In fact, he is ashamed not so much of his body as precisely of lust" (TB, 116).

8b. Shame also has a positive meaning as "a natural form of self-defense for the person against the danger of descending or being pushed into the position of an object for sexual use" (LR, 182).

8c. "The 'heart' has become a battlefield between love and lust. The more lust dominates the heart, the less the [heart] experiences the nuptial meaning of the body" (TB, 126).

 POINTS TO PONDER

How is lust (disordered sexual desire) manifested differently in men and women? Why is pornography viewed primarily by men? Why are romance novels read primarily by women? Do these offer a realistic portrayal of man and woman's relationship? Are they an aid to teaching us the meaning of self-giving love?

84-86

175

Summary:
What's It Mean for Our Marriage?

• God created us male and female and calls us to "be fruitful and multiply" in order to reveal his own mystery of love and enable us to participate in it.

• This means that marriage can only satisfy our deep longing for love and union to the degree that it images God's love.

• The sin of our first parents disoriented man and woman's desire for each other. Men and women must now resist the selfish sting of lust and the tendency to use each other if they are to experience the happiness for which they long.

Purpose of this talk:

- to provide an overview of Christ's redemptive work in restoring man and woman's relationship according to God's original plan;
- to help couples understand that there is real power in Christ to live according to their deepest desires for love and intimacy in marriage;
- to call couples to conversion in Christ, encouraging them to dedicate their lives and their marriage to him as the sure means to happiness in marriage;
- to witness personally to the power of Christ in your own life (and your own marriage, if married).

Logistics: This talk should last 40 minutes.

Note: The miracle at Cana is extremely rich in meaning. Lacking time for a thorough exegesis of the passage, the main point is to demonstrate to the couples that if they would but invite Christ to their marriage (as did the couple at Cana), he would work a miracle in their lives as well. Every couple has "run out of wine" (God's love in their hearts) because of original sin. True joy in marriage comes from loving as Christ loves, but this can only happen if we allow Christ to purify our hearts. It can only happen if we drink deeply from the "new wine" that Christ gives us.

Christ Restores God's Plan for Marriage:

Male & Female He Redeemed Them

1. Christ's First Miracle

27-28

DVD○
SEGMENT 1: *2:30*
Review of Talk One

It is of utmost significance that Christ performed his first public miracle at a (1) _____wedding_____.

DVD○
SEGMENT 2: *3:15*
Christ Restores God's
Plan for Marriage

> On the third day, there was a marriage at Cana in Galilee, and the mother of Jesus was there; Jesus was also invited to the marriage, with his disciples. When the wine failed, the mother of Jesus said to him, "They have no wine." And Jesus said to her, "O woman, what have you to do with me? My hour has not yet come." His mother said to the servants, "Do whatever he tells you." Now six stone jars were standing there, for the Jewish rites of purification, each holding twenty or thirty gallons. Jesus said to them, "Fill the jars with water." And they filled them up to the brim. He said to them "Now draw some out, and take it to the steward of the feast. ...The water [had] now become wine (Jn 2:1-9).

Wine is a symbol of God's (2) _____love_____. "Running out of wine" seems to indicate that...

1a. "Without [Christ's] help man and woman cannot achieve the union of their lives for which God created them 'in the beginning'" (CCC, n. 1608).

While we might sense a deep longing in our hearts for the original harmony of the sexes, God's original plan for marriage often seems like pie-in-the-sky idealism. Is it possible to live it?

- Christ came into the world for this specific reason: to restore the "wine" of God's love in superabundance. This is why the Gospel is *good news*.

- Because of the distortions of sin in our hearts, loving rightly is a difficult struggle. But if we drink deeply from the "new wine" that Christ gives us, we have a sure path to a "joy-filled" marriage.

Suggestion: It's always helpful to appeal to couple's experience in making these points. Men and women know that they're not meant to be used. Women, in particular, know the feeling of being violated by another man's lustful "look." The tragic thing is that we often call lust "love" because it is all we've known. The heart knows better, and we must not settle for counterfeit versions of love.

Note: This is a delicate point that needs careful explanation so that couples don't think that sexual attraction itself is somehow inappropriate. What is wrong is lustful attraction — the impulse to use one's spouse merely as a means of selfish pleasure. Authentic sexual attraction desires to uphold the other's true beauty and dignity as a person made in God's image. Weeding out lust does not diminish sexual attraction, but enhances and enriches it.

Note: This is precisely the key to a thoroughly Christian view of marriage — marital love and the attraction of the sexes have been redeemed in Christ! If this is not the central point that we are seeking to convey to engaged couples and inviting them to embrace, all we can offer them are various coping mechanisms for the "hardness of heart" that makes marriage so difficult. We must be able to witness to the authentic liberation that comes from allowing Christ to transform our hearts. See video for suggestions.

1b. "By coming to restore the original order of creation disturbed by sin, [Christ] himself gives the strength and grace to... 'receive' the original meaning of marriage and live it" (CCC, n. 1615).

2. Christ Takes Us to the Heart of the Matter

27

DVD●
SEGMENT 3: *6:15*
Christ Takes Us to
the Heart of the
Matter: Love vs. Lust

"You have heard that it was said, 'You shall not commit adultery.' But I say to you that everyone who looks at a woman lustfully has already committed adultery with her in his heart" (Mt 5:27-28).

103-104

- Marriage *does not justify lust.* Lust, in fact, is the main enemy of true married love, the root cause in a sense of all marital disharmony.

- The opposite of love is not hatred. The opposite of love is to *use* someone as a means to my own selfish end. The opposite of love is *lust.*

74-76

- Therefore, if spouses are to experience true, lasting joy in their marriage, they must work diligently with God's help to overcome the selfish "sting" of lust.

2a. Liberation from lust "is the condition of all life together in the truth" (TB, 158-159).

2b. "Adultery in the heart is committed not only because man 'looks' in this way at a woman who is not his wife.... Even if he looked in this way at his wife, he could likewise commit adultery 'in his heart'" (TB, 157).

2c. Are we to fear the severity of these words, or rather have confidence in their power to save us (see TB, 159)?

2d. Christ calls us to experience "a real and deep victory" over the distortion of lust (see TB, 164). Christ wants to in-spire sexual desire "with everything that is noble and beautiful," with "the supreme value which is love" (see TB, 168).

DVD●
SEGMENT 4: *5:00*
The Redemption of
Human Sexuality

Through ongoing conversion of our hearts to Christ, we come gradually to experience sexual desire as the desire to love as God loves: freely, totally, faithfully, and fruitfully. This means we can experience the (3) ___redemption___ of our sexual desires.

82-84

POINTS TO PONDER

If Christ has restored God's original plan for sexual desire as the norm, and truly gives us the power to live it, why, then, do so few people seem to be living it? What can I do, personally, to enter more fully into a transformed or "redeemed" experience of sexual attraction and desire?

Note: Before discussing Ephesians 5, it's very important to acknowledge the controversy that surrounds this passage. It's interesting to note that the passage that John Paul II calls the "summa, in some sense, of the teaching about God and man" also contains one of the most controversial verses in the Bible ("wives submit to your husbands"). On the one hand, since the verse is most often thought to justify male domination, it's important to affirm people's rightful opposition to this idea. On the other hand, while all of St. Paul's letters should be read in light of the culture and time in which he lived, it's important not to dismiss his words as a mere product of his culture. St. Paul, in calling spouses to a "mutual subjection" out of "reverence for Christ" is actually being extremely counter-cultural. He is seeking to restore God's original plan of love between man and woman by comparing it to the love between Christ and the Church. When we understand this, it turns the typical interpretation of this passage on its head. See video for suggestions in presentation.

3. Liberation from Lust Sets Us Free from the Law

65-66 **DVD●** NOTES
SEGMENT 5: *9:15*
Beyond the Law:
The Experience of
Freedom in Christ

You "were called to freedom... if you are led by the Spirit, you are not under the law" (Gal 5:13, 18).

- How many people think that being a Christian means following a long list of oppressive rules?

- Christ did not come to give us more "rules" to follow; he came to change our hearts so that we would no longer need the rules.

- In effect Christ says, "You've heard the commandment not to commit adultery, but the problem is you *desire* to commit adultery."

- Here's where the Gospel becomes *good news:* If we let him in, Christ can change our hearts to the point that we become "free from the law" — not free to break it, but free to fulfill it.

- True freedom is liberation not from the *external* "constraint" that calls me to good, but from the *internal* constraint that hinders my choice of the good.

3a. Those bound by lust "experience God's law as a burden, and indeed as ...a restriction of their own freedom. On the other hand, those who are impelled by love ...feel an interior urge... not to stop at the minimum demands of the Law, but to live them in their 'fullness.' This is a still uncertain and fragile journey as long as we are on earth, but it is one made possible by grace" (VS, n. 18)

3b. "The Law of the Gospel ...does not add new external precepts, but proceeds to reform the heart" (CCC, n. 1968). In "the Sermon on the Mount ...the Spirit of the Lord gives new form to our desires" (CCC, n. 2764).

4. Liberation from Lust Leads to "Reverence for Christ"

DVD●
SEGMENT 6: *7:30*
Ephesians Chapter 5:
Mutual Submission
in Christ

61-63

"Be subject to one another out of reverence for Christ. As the church is subject to Christ, so let wives also be subject in everything to their husbands. Husbands, love your wives, as Christ loved the church and gave himself up for her" (Eph 5:21, 24-25).

- According to the analogy, the wife is a symbol of the Church and the husband is a symbol of Christ.

- Christ came not to *be* served *but to serve* — to lay down his life for his Bride (see Mt 20:28).

- St. Paul *does not justify male domination.* This is the result of sin (see Gen 3:16). St. Paul is seeking to restore the original order *before* sin.

- When St. Paul calls wives to "submit" to their husbands, he's saying, "Wives, allow your husbands to (4) _____serve_____ you by pouring their lives in love and care for you."

4a. Since the "submission of the Church to Christ …consists in experiencing his love," we can conclude that "the wife's 'submission' to her husband … signifies above all 'the experiencing of love'" (TB, 320).

4b. That "reverence for Christ" St. Paul speaks of is none other than a spiritually mature form of the mutual attraction of the sexes (see TB, 379).

4c. If a husband is truly to love his wife, "it is necessary to insist that intercourse must not serve merely as a means of allowing [his] climax. …The man must take [the] difference between male and female reactions into account …so that climax may be reached [by] both …and as far as possible occur in both simultaneously." The husband must do this "not for hedonistic, but for altruistic reasons." In this case, if "we take into account the shorter and more violent curve of arousal in the man, [such] tenderness on his part in the context of marital intercourse acquires the significance of an act of virtue" (LR, 272, 275).

5. How Do We Live a Redeemed Marriage?

If the source of all of the problems of man and woman's relationship is the fact that we have doubted God's love for us and turned our back on him, then what would the solution be?

69-70
82-84
100-102

- We must (5) _____return_____ to God. Christ's first words of his public ministry were, "Repent and believe the good news!" (Mk 1:15).

29

- We must invite Christ into our lives as our Redeemer and allow him to convert our hearts. We must say "yes" to God's marriage proposal.

- As members of the Church, we must submit to Christ as our Bridegroom, abandoning ourselves to his love for us and pledging our love to him in return.

This means spending time with Christ in daily *prayer*, getting to know him by reading his *word* and living a (6) _____sacramental_____ life.

Suggestion: The close of this talk could be devoted to a personal testimony of Christ's work in your own life and marriage (if you're married) and a clear invitation to the couples to entrust their lives and their marriages to Christ. The private reflection exercise to follow will help them consider this invitation. Your personal witness to Christ is indispensable in bringing the contents of the class to the level of practical implementation for the couples.

• Living a sacramental life means embracing the faith we received in *Baptism*, being reconciled to Christ and his Church when we fall through *Confession,* and being fed each Sunday (and more often when possible) in the *Eucharist.*

DVD◉   **NOTES**
SEGMENT 7: *5:45*
A Lesson in Trust

 POINTS TO PONDER

As C.S. Lewis once said, "Christianity, if false, is of no importance; and if true, of infinite importance. The one thing it cannot be is moderately important." Following Christ is a radical call. Christ himself encouraged us to "count the cost" before beginning the journey (see Lk 14:28-33). But he also promised an eternal inheritance for those who "sold everything" to follow him. Ponder the following words of Christ. What bearing do they have on your future marriage?

"If any man would come after me, let him deny himself and take up his cross daily and follow me. For whoever would save his life will lose it; and whoever loses his life for my sake, he will save it. For what does it profit a man if he gains the whole world and loses or forfeits himself?" (Lk 9:23-25).

"Fear not, little flock, for it is your Father's good pleasure to give you the Kingdom. Sell your possessions and give alms; provide yourselves with purses that do not grow old, with a treasure in heaven that does not fail, where no thief approaches and no moth destroys. For where your treasure is, there your heart will be also" (Lk 12:32-34).

"If you love me, you will keep my commandments" (Jn 14:15).

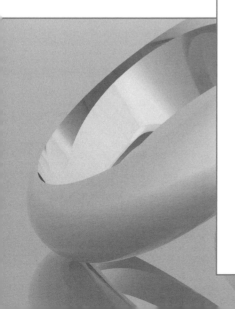

Summary
What's It Mean for Our Marriage?

• The *good news* of the Gospel is that Christ came into the world to restore God's original plan for marriage. If we drink the "new wine" that Christ offers every married couple, we really can experience the love and happiness we long for.

• Living God's plan for marriage does not mean following a long list of oppressive rules. To the degree that we allow Christ to transform our hearts, we experience "freedom from the law" — not as license to break God's law, but as an interior yearning to live God's plan for marriage to the full.

• Because of the selfish sting of original sin in each of us, marital love is in need of redemption, healing, transformation. Experiencing this transformation begins by entrusting our lives and our relationship entirely to Christ.

Purpose of this exercise:

- to help participants reflect individually and later as a couple on the importance of Christ in their lives and their relationship;

- to help each person pray in a way that corresponds to where he or she honestly is in his or her relationship with God.

Logistics: Read the following "Note on the Goal of this Exercise" aloud so that everyone understands what to do. Read also the note under "Honest Prayers." Suggest that they simply put a check next to the prayer they choose. In order to encourage freedom of thought, separate the couples by having the men go to one side of the room and the women to the other. Give everyone approximately fifteen minutes to reflect. Ask them not to return to their places until you direct them in order to provide a quiet atmosphere for others. If your schedule permits, time can be allotted for the couples to share their reflections then. If not, then they could do so over lunch or on their own time after the class.

Private Reflection Exercise

Note on the Goal of this Exercise

Throughout this class you will be given opportunities such as this to reflect on various ideas and questions that are of importance to your relationship — first, individually, by writing in your workbook, and then by sharing what you've written with your fiancé(e). If you aren't used to writing down your thoughts, you may find it doesn't come easily at first. We encourage you to stick with it and just write down whatever comes to mind. Once you get started you'll find it gets easier. This method of reflection has proven to be a very effective way of stimulating thoughtful communication on topics that sometimes remain inadequately addressed otherwise. This is your chance to address honestly some issues of the "heart"— your own heart, and the heart you share as a couple. It may take some effort, but it's sure to pay off in the many ways it will help you grow in your love for and understanding of one another.

1. *What's my perspective? Why?*

Many couples coming to the Church today for the sacrament of marriage, although they may have been raised in the Church, have stopped practicing their faith. They often have sincere questions and doubts about the relevance of Christianity to their every day lives and their future marriage. Perhaps religion just seems like a bunch of oppressive rules and they've never really heard or understood what it means to **know Christ personally and play an active role in the Church.**

2.   *What do I think about saying "yes" to God's proposal and entrusting my life and my marriage to Christ? What feelings does this idea conjure up in me — anxiety, peace, resistance, excitement, fear, joy? Why?*

God loves us beyond our wildest-dreams and he wants more than anything to shower us with his love and grant us his own eternal life. Heaven is the eternal marriage between Christ and his Bride, the Church. Applying this analogy, we learn that God wants to "marry" us. In fact, God created marriage as a way for us to share in his love on earth and prepare us for the marriage to come in heaven. But heaven isn't automatic. Like any good husband, God respects our freedom and never forces himself on us. He only holds out a "proposal" and it's up to us to accept it or reject it.

Honest Prayers

All of us are at different places in our relationship with God.

Hopefully one or more of the following prayers will be helpful to you in your situation.

Pick the prayer that most honestly expresses your heart and share why with your fiance(é).

God, if you exist...

Dear God, I don't even know if you exist. I feel strange even asking at the risk that I'm praying to nobody. If you're there, please hear my prayer. Please, somehow, let me know that you are real and that you love me. And teach me how to love you in return. Amen. ""

God, I know you're there, but...

Dear God, I know you're there, but I'm afraid to surrender my life and our relationship to you. I'm afraid of what you might ask of me, what I may need to change or give up. If you are all-loving, I know I shouldn't be afraid, but I am. Forgive me. Give me the grace to trust you with my whole life and with our relationship. Amen. ""

God, I reaffirm my commitment to you...

Dear God, thank you for the great gift of sharing in your love and your life. I reaffirm my commitment to you and ask you to draw me ever deeper into your infinite love. Jesus, you know I am not perfect. You know my failings, my weaknesses, and my sins. Yet you love me unconditionally. Help me so that my life might reflect that love more perfectly. I place my life and our entire relationship in your hands. Give us the grace to remain always faithful to you and to each other. Amen. ""

God, I give you my life...

Dear God, I believe that you love me and desire only what is best for me. Jesus, since you came to give up your life for me, I, now, want to live my life for you. I'm sorry for the ways that I have turned from you in the past. I'm sorry for the ways that I have not let you into my life and into our relationship. Jesus, I believe that you died for me so that I could live a new life. I accept this great gift of your love, and from this day on, I want to live as you are calling me to live. Show me the way. I give you my whole life. I give you our relationship. Teach us what it means to love each other as you love us so that our marriage might be what you want it to be. Amen. ""

God, I recommit my life to you...

Dear God, you know I once committed my life to you, but have fallen away. Forgive me for losing sight of your infinite love for me. Forgive me for choosing my own path instead of following you. I recommit my life to you. I give our entire relationship to you. Just as I desire to be faithful to my future spouse, I desire to be faithful to you. Lord, you know I am weak. Grant me the grace never to turn from you again. Thank you for welcoming me back into your arms. Amen. ""

Purpose of this talk:

- to define marriage and help couples understand what makes marriage a sacrament;
- to reflect on the meaning of the vows, helping couples understand what they're committing to;
- to introduce couples to the teaching of canon law regarding marriage — for example: what makes a marriage valid, what an annulment is (and is not), the meaning of consummation, etc.

Logistics: This talk should last approximately 40 minutes.

Note: The Catholic Church makes a distinction between a sacramental marriage and a good and natural one. The marriage between two baptized Christians, often referred to as holy matrimony, is a sacrament. The marriage of two unbaptized people or of one baptized and one unbaptized person is not a sacramental marriage, but a "good and natural marriage." This point may arise in your discussion with couples.

Suggestion: It's important to spend a few minutes giving a brief catechesis on the sacraments. You can assume some general knowledge from the audience, but few will understand what a sacrament actually is — a bodily, sensual encounter with God and a sharing in his life and grace. Some may know that sacraments concern signs and symbols, but few will understand that these signs actually communicate what they signify. Teaching on the sensual, bodily nature of the sacraments is also an excellent opportunity to counter the widespread error that living a "spiritual" life means rejecting the body. Christ becomes "one flesh" with his Bride, the Church, by virtue of the Incarnation itself. In fact, as various saints and popes have confirmed, the union of man and woman in "one flesh" was a foreshadowing, right from the beginning, of the Incarnation. Furthermore, in the Eucharist, the Church unites herself to Christ in such a way that we become "one spirit, one body with Christ" (Eucharistic prayer).

Note: In Churches of the Eastern rite, the priest is considered the minister of the sacrament of marriage.

Suggestion: In eliciting answers to numbers 5 and 6, it would be helpful first to give examples of the form and matter of other sacraments. Eucharist: form = words of consecration, and matter = bread and wine. Baptism: form = baptismal formula, and matter = water. If the words of consecration or the baptismal formula are changed, it's not a valid sacrament. Similarly, you can't have a valid Eucharist by consecrating graham crackers and beer or a valid Baptism by bathing someone with tar. You can lighten the discussion by recognizing that these technicalities are probably more than they ever wanted to know about sacraments. The importance of understanding the form and matter of marriage, however, will make sense as the discussion continues. As always, you can see the video for suggested approaches

---

What Are You Saying "I Do" to?

45-64

The Basics of Marriage in the Church

1. Defining Marriage

Since "God himself is the author of marriage" (CCC, n. 1603), we are not free to change it at will. Marriage is only marriage to the extent that it conforms to God's design for it.

1a. Marriage is the intimate, exclusive, indissoluble communion of life and love entered by man and woman at the design of the Creator for the purpose of their own good and the procreation and education of children; this covenant between baptized persons has been raised by Christ the Lord to the dignity of a sacrament (see CCC, n. 1601 and CCL, can. 1055).

46-47

2. What Makes Marriage a Sacrament?

47-49

Sacraments are visible signs in the world that truly communicate God's invisible mystery of life and love to us. Sacraments, you might say, are where heaven and earth "kiss," where Christ becomes one with his Bride in and through our (1) _____flesh_____.

The purpose of the sacraments is to unite us with Christ our Bridegroom in an eternal, life-giving bond of love. Marriage, then, is not only one of the seven sacraments, but, according to John Paul II, it is in some sense the (2) _____prototype_____ of all the sacraments (see TB, 339).

2a. "The entire Christian life bears the mark of the spousal love of Christ and the Church. Already Baptism...is a nuptial mystery; it is so to speak the nuptial bath which precedes the wedding feast, the Eucharist" (CCC, n. 1617).

The (3) _____bride_____ and _____groom_____ are the ministers of the sacrament of marriage which is brought about by the free exchange of consent (the wedding vows). The priest or deacon serves only as an official (4) _____witness_____ for the Church (see CCC, n. 1623).

50-52

For sacraments to be celebrated validly they must have proper "form" (this refers to the words spoken) and "matter" (the physical reality). The exchange of (5) _____vows_____ properly witnessed

Note: The four qualities of God's love outlined in the first talk (free, total, faithful, and fruitful) and discussed throughout *Good News About Sex & Marriage* form the essence of the questions of intention to marry. It's important to stress that at the altar couples are simply committing to love one another as God loves.

Note: Annulment cases from diocesan tribunals indicate that many people who marry in the Church today don't adequately understand what they are committing to. Many lament that had they only known ahead of time what it means to marry in the Church, they might have been spared a lot of pain and disillusionment. This talk is meant to prevent such disillusionment by informing couples "ahead of time." It will be helpful to the couples to acknowledge that a discussion of Church law on marriage can seem rather "dry" and "technical." Nonetheless, to ensure the valid celebration of marriage, it's very important for couples to understand "the basics."

Note: This portion of the talk lays important groundwork for Part II of the class. It is crucial for couples to understand why genital intercourse consummates marriage. Since couples have been raised in a society that has severed sex from its inherent marital meaning, it is crucial for couples to understand that genital intercourse — as God created it to be — is meant to express and renew the wedding vows. Whatever you can do as an instructor to help this point "sink in" will aid couples greatly in understanding God's plan for sexual union.

by the Church is the form, and the very (6) _____bodies_____ of husband and wife make up the matter of the sacrament of marriage.

3. The Exchange of Consent

20
53

DVD⊙
SEGMENT 3: *4:15*
The Exchange of Consent

The priest or deacon will ask you three "Questions of Intention to Marry." They are:

- *Have you come here **freely** and **without reservation** to give yourselves to each other in marriage? (Bride & groom respond "I have.")*

- *Will you love and honor each other as man and wife for the **rest of your lives**? (Bride & Groom respond "I will.")*

- *Will you **accept children** lovingly from God, and bring them up according to the law of Christ and his Church? (Bride & Groom respond "I will.")*

> **POINTS TO PONDER**
> Is it possible for people to consent to these questions of intention to marry without meaning what they say? Would they still be married if they did?

50-54

Then the priest or deacon will say:

Since it is your intention to enter into marriage, join your right hands and declare your consent before God and his Church.

You will then declare your consent:

I, _____, take you, _____, to be my wife/husband. I promise to be true to you in good times and in bad, in sickness and in health. I will love you and honor you all the days of my life.

4. The Definitive Expression of Married Love

20

DVD⊙
SEGMENT 4: *6:45*
Sex: The Difinitive Expression
of Married Love

Marriage is brought about by the free exchange of consent properly witnessed by the Church. However, marriage is not (7) _____consummated_____ that is, perfected, sealed, and brought to completion — until the spouses...

4a. "...have performed between themselves in a human manner the conjugal act which is per se suitable for the generation of children" (CCL, can. 1061).

Suggestion: This point is worth elaborating upon. Uniting sexually is not just something that married people happen to do. Sexual union expresses — or is meant to express — what marriage is: the free, total, faithful, and fruitful self-giving of man and woman to each other. Far from being a limited "event" or "moment" in the course of married life, sexual intercourse serves as a summation (con-summation) of the whole of married life. It is a window into the heart and reality of marriage. As the body expresses and reveals the soul of a person, so does sexual intercourse express and reveal the "soul" of married life. Thus, if sexual union is not lived according to God's plan, it will have a damaging impact on the whole of a couple's married life.

This technical definition from the *Code of Canon Law* is obviously not the most romantic way to talk about sex, but in our day of widespread sexual confusion, it's important to have a precise understanding of what does and does not consummate a marriage.

- Genital intercourse is called the "conjugal act" or the "marital embrace" because it's the definitive expression of the marriage commitment. It's a sign that encompasses and sums up the whole reality of the joining of two lives in marriage.

  55

- When a husband and wife consummate their marriage, the "form" and "matter" of the sacrament are united. The words of the wedding vows become (8) _____flesh_____.

- This means every time a husband and wife have sexual intercourse they're meant to be expressing and (9) _____renewing_____ their wedding vows.

  87-91

4b. Marital "consent ...finds its fulfillment in the two 'becoming one flesh'" (CCC, n. 1627).

 POINTS TO PONDER

If sexual intercourse is the defining element of marital love, how might the definition of marriage be affected by a redefinition of sexual intercourse?

54-57
107-108

5. What Makes Marriage Valid?

Marriage is not something that automatically "happens" to a couple by virtue of going through the motions of a ceremony. Marriage only "happens" if a bride and groom validly minister the sacrament to each other.

50-58

DVD
SEGMENT 5: *8:30*
What Makes
Marriage Valid?

- Numerous things can and sometimes do impede the valid celebration of a marriage. Thus, it's very important to understand what makes a marriage valid and what might impede it from being so.

- A declaration of nullity, (commonly referred to as an "annulment"), is not a Catholic version of divorce, but an official statement that a valid marriage never, in fact, existed. Divorce, in the sense of ending a valid marriage, is always an impossibility.

Note: Impediments are saved for the final portion of this talk because the impediment of impotence, in particular, generally necessitates careful explanation. This is best saved for last.

Suggestion: You may want to point out here that these ages not only reflect the universality of the Church (i.e. it's normal in some cultures for men and women to marry this young, but it would not be recommended in our culture), but they also reflect the different ages of sexual maturity in men and women.

In order for a marriage to be validly established, bride and   50-53
groom must:

→ • *not have any (10)* _____ impediments _____ *to marriage; See below...*

• *follow the proper (11)* _____ form _____ *of the sacrament;*

> This means (unless a dispensation is granted) you must have your exchange of vows witnessed by an official minister of the Church and two other witnesses. It also means you cannot alter the vows. For example, you could not say, "I promise to be true to you in good times, but not bad ...and only for the next three years at which time we will re-evaluate."

• *have the proper capacity to exchange consent and do so (12)* _____ freely _____ *and* _____ unconditionally _____ :

This means if either party is hampered psychologically, or offers consent under fear or duress, or places any condition on the marriage (I'll only stay married if...), then marriage is not contracted.

• *consent to what the Church intends by marriage, that is: (13)* _____ fidelity _____ , _____ indissolubility _____ , *and openness to* _____ children _____ .

5a. "The Church holds the exchange of consent between the spouses to be the indispensable element that 'makes the marriage.' If consent is lacking there is no marriage" (CCC, n. 1626).

Impediments to marriage include (see CCL, cans. 1083-1094):

→ • men under age 16 and women under age 14;

• pre-existence of a valid marriage;

• persons bound by perpetual vows to remain celibate (e.g. priests and religious);

• persons who have brought about the death of their spouses in order to marry;

• persons who have abducted their fiancé(e) for the purpose of marriage;

• close relatives whether by blood or adoption;

DVD⊙
SEGMENT 6: *3:45*
Impediments to
Marriage in
the Church

Note: The fact that impotence is an impediment to marriage often surprises people. It even rouses anger in some. Difficulty in understanding why the impossibility of sexual intercourse would render marriage impossible stems, once again, from the severance of sex from its inherent marital meaning. It is strongly recommended that you are well versed in addressing people's objections to this impediment in a thoughtful manner. It is also important to clarify that impotence is not an impediment because children are impossible (natural infertility is *not* an impediment to marriage). It is an impediment because consummation is impossible. See *Good News About Sex & Marriage*, pages 54-57.

- definitive and perpetual impotence (inability to consummate marriage).

 POINTS TO PONDER

It's often said that sex isn't everything in a marriage. That's true in some sense. But why is the ability to have marital intercourse essential to the ability to marry?

Summary

What's It Mean for Our Marriage?

- Getting married in the Catholic Church presupposes that you intend what the Catholic Church intends by marriage. That is, you intend to enter a Sacrament (if you are both baptized) and live, with God's help, the commitments of fidelity, indissolubility, and openness to children.

- Marriage takes place at the moment bride and groom exchange consent according to the form of the Church. Marital consent is brought to fulfillment when the spouses express the defining element of marriage in conjugal intercourse.

- Marriage does not happen "automatically." Various factors can and sometimes do impede the valid celebration of the sacrament. It is therefore extremely important that a couple understand what makes marriage valid in the eyes of the Church.

Private Reflection Exercise

Why do I want to get married?

_____

_____

_____

_____

These may seem like simple or basic questions, but they serve as a platform for addressing issues of central importance. Don't be satisfied with quick answers. **Dig deep!**

_____

_____

_____

_____

_____

_____

_____

_____

_____

_____

_____

_____

_____

_____

_____

_____

_____

_____

_____

_____

_____

Why do I want to marry you?

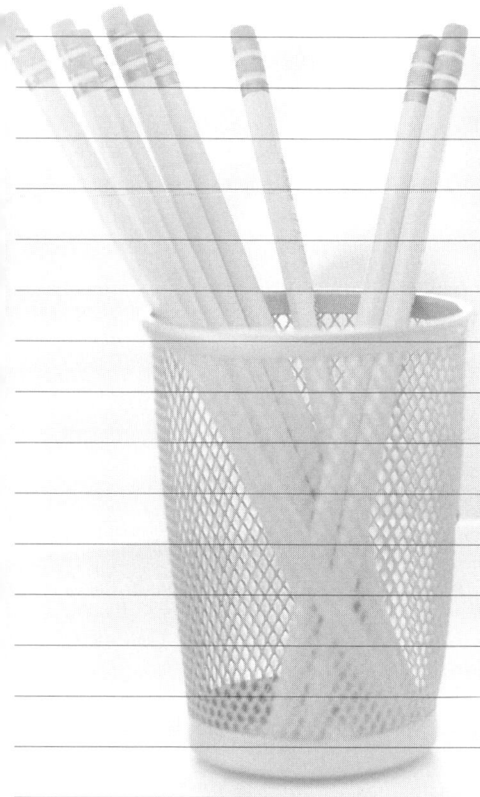

_____

_____

_____

_____

_____

_____

_____

_____

_____

_____

_____

_____

_____

_____

_____

_____

_____

_____

_____

_____

_____

_____

_____

_____

_____

_____

_____

_____

Do I intend what the Catholic Church intends by marriage?

Why do I want to get married in the Catholic Church?

Note: Widespread abandonment of God's plan for sexual union lies at the heart of the modern breakdown of marriage and family life. Hence, the Sacramental Sexuality session of the program is of utmost importance in preparing couples to embrace "God's plan for a joy-filled marriage."

The following talks involve frank discussion of Church teaching about sexual morality. Recognizing that an open discussion of sexual matters might be difficult for some participants in the class, it's important to put people at ease. Above all, it's important that you are at ease in discussing the topic. Couples have a right to know what the Church really teaches and why. As catechists in this area, we have an obligation to speak forthrightly: with delicacy and prudence, to be sure, but without avoidance. Silence feeds ignorance, and ignorance is unaffordable if couples are to embrace "God's plan for a joy-filled marriage."

The effects on the engaged of living in a culture that bombards them with a vision of sexuality antithetical to God's plan cannot be underestimated. In a survey of approximately 2,000 people who attended this class, 91% were already sexually active. On the bright side, after the Church's teaching was clearly presented and explained to these couples and a direct challenge was lovingly extended to embrace it, 48% of them indicated that they "definitely" planned on refraining from sex until marriage. Another 20% indicated that they were "considering it."

Pastoral experience also attests that many engaged persons have had sexual experiences (sometimes numerous ones) prior to meeting their fiancé(e). Whenever people engage in sexual activity that is not an expression of marriage, they injure their ability to experience true sexual intimacy when they do marry. If the wounds caused by such experiences are left unaddressed, they can actually cripple a couple from living and loving as God intends. Hence, there is a crucial need in marriage preparation to help couples who are wounded from illicit sexual experiences to at least begin the process of healing.

Furthermore, it must be recognized that at the heart of the widespread abandonment of God's plan for sexuality lies the severance of sexual union from its ordination towards procreation. Far from being peripheral, the Church's constant and unchangeable teaching that "each and every marriage act must remain open to the transmission of life" is essential to the nature and meaning of marriage. In fact, by accepting contraception, the internal logic of the sacramentality of marriage collapses. Thus, helping couples understand and embrace the wisdom of the Church's teaching against contraception is one of the most important goals of this class. A significant portion of the second presentation will be devoted to this issue.

Part II:

Sacramental *Sexuality*

If we're ever to discover true love, true joy, true happiness, we must rediscover the "nuptial meaning of the body" and live according to it.

GN, p. 85

Purpose of this talk:

- to help couples understand how they have been conditioned to think about sex by their upbringing and by society, and to learn to evaluate it critically;
- to help couples distinguish authentic love and lust;
- to help couples understand what it means to be sexually honest before marriage, emphasizing the joy such honesty brings without minimizing the challenge it involves;
- to extend a direct challenge for those who are sexually active to save sex until it can be an honest expression of their marriage commitment;
- to encourage those couples who have been sexually active with others to begin the healing process necessary to live a fruitful marriage unencumbered by the past;
- to hold out Christ's gift of grace which truly empowers us, despite our weaknesses, to live the truth.

Logistics: This talk should last approximately 40 minutes.

Suggestion: To help couples evaluate society's message about sex, contrast some of the promises of the sexual revolution (for example, better relations between the sexes, better marriages, healthier families, carefree sex, liberation, etc.) with what has actually happened (dramatic increases in rates of adultery, divorce, rape, date rape, other sexual abuse, sexual addiction, sexually transmitted diseases, abortion, domestic violence, psychological trauma, fatherless children, etc., etc. – is this liberation?). Furthermore, to help the couples evaluate the message communicated by their own families about sex, review the following Points to Ponder aloud with the class. Share with the group some of your experiences and impressions growing up and what helped you come to understand and embrace God's plan for sexuality in your own life.

Suggestion: This section, when properly presented, rings true in the human heart in a particular way. Who can deny that the human person is looking to be loved, affirmed, and received as a unique and unrepeatable gift? The goal here is to help couples "connect" with this desire within and to demonstrate that sex only corresponds to our dignity and our deepest longings when it expresses love for the "unrepeatability" of the person.

The Joy of Sexual Honesty Before Marriage

DVD●
SEGMENT 1: *1:15*
Review of
Morning Talk   **NOTES**

DVD●
SEGMENT 2: *11:30*
The Joy of Sexual
Honesty Before Marriage

DVD●
SEGMENT 3: *8:00*
Sex, Lies and the
Language of the Culture

1. Sex, Lies, & Culture

We live in a world saturated with information about sex. No one who has grown up in our culture is unaffected by the barrage of sexual images, messages, and innuendos communicated through TV, movies, magazines, billboards, and more recently the Internet.

- All of this has a deep and lasting impact on the way we think of ourselves, the way we view our bodies, how we understand the meaning of sex, and, yes, on the way we think about, pursue, enter, and live in (1) _____marriage_____.

- In order to experience the true joy of sex as God intends for us, it's important to look at how we've been formed to think about sex, by our own families and by society.

 POINTS TO PONDER

· Where did you learn about sex for the first time?

· Was there open, honest communication in your family about sex? If not, why not?

· What impressions did you have of your own body as you experienced puberty?

100-102

2. Signs of a Mature Sexual Love

DVD●
SEGMENT 4: *12:00*
Signs of Mature Sexual Love

How are we to distinguish between authentic love and lust?

72-79
93
105

2a. Lust "is not always plain and obvious; sometimes it is concealed, so that it passes itself off as 'love'" (TB, 126).

2b. Lust impels people very powerfully towards physical intimacy. But if this grows out of nothing more than lust it is not love. On the contrary it is a negation of love (see LR, 150-151).

Love reaches maturity when it turns from how the other makes me feel to who the other person is.

- Every person is totally unique and (2) _____unrepeatable_____.

- No person can ever be compared to another, measured by, or replaced by another. Authentic love is attracted not just by "attributes" or "qualities" of a person that light a "spark."

- Qualities are *repeatable* — they can always be found in others and to a higher degree. If love stops here, a permanent shadow is cast over the permanency of relationship.

2c. "Only the value of the person can sustain a stable relationship. The other values of sexuality are wasted away by time and are exposed to the danger of disillusion. But this is not the case for the value of the person, ...which is stable and in some way infinite. When love develops and reaches the person, then it is forever" (KW, 100).

The person who is the object of lust gradually realizes the sentiment of the other:

- "You don't need *me*. You don't desire *me*. You desire only a means of gratification."

- Far from feeling loved and affirmed as a unique and unrepeatable person, those objectified by lust feel used and debased as a repeatable commodity.

2d. We often experience sexual stimuli offering equally or more seductive possibilities of new sexual relationships. If the person I "love" is only an instrument for my own pleasure, then he or she can easily be replaced in that function, a fact which casts a permanent shadow of doubt over the relationship. The case is different when love reaches the person. Then the other is loved not for the quality that he or she has (and which one can lose or which others could have in a higher degree) but for his or her own sake. Only then is their living together something more than the joining of two selfish individuals, and capable of achieving a real personal unity (see KW, 102).

Suggestion: It will be helpful to have familiarized yourself with the "psychology" of sex outside marriage and why it is so detrimental to a couple when they do marry (see *Good News About Sex & Marriage*, pages 71-73).

3. What is Sexual Honesty?

DVD● NOTES
SEGMENT 5: *7:00*
What is Sexual Honesty?

Sexual honesty means:

- accepting and respecting the (3) _____language_____ of love
that God inscribed in our bodies when he created us in his own
image as male and female;   66-68

- learning to love as God loves in all our expressions of affection and   20
intimacy;

- above all, never (4) _____using_____ another person
(in thought or action) as a means of sexual gratification.   74-76

 POINTS TO PONDER

This last statement does *not* mean that sexual pleasure is bad. However,   41
God created it to be experienced as the joy of loving as he loves, not   75
sought as an end in itself. How would it affect a spouse if he or she were   97-98
treated merely as a means to an orgasm?   103-104

We all recognize that the body possesses a language. We also
recognize that it's possible to contradict this language, to speak a lie
with the body. For example:

- A used car salesman who knows he just sold you a lemon speaks a
lie when he looks you in the eye and shakes your hand.

- When Judas kissed Jesus in the garden of Gethsemane, he used an
expression of affection as an act of betrayal.

(5) _____Truth_____ and _____love_____ go hand
in hand. Lying is a contradiction of love. It simply can never be an act
of true love to speak a lie with the body.

4. The Joy & the Challenge

Sexual honesty brings true joy because it expresses true love. But
this joy also comes at a high price. Sexual honesty presents a serious   41
challenge, particularly in today's world in which sex has been virtually
sapped of its inherent (6) _____marital_____ meaning.

Because we've all been so deeply affected by society's sexual   69-74
confusion, *coming to understand and embrace God's plan for sexual*

Note: Now is the opportune time to issue a direct challenge for all those who are sexually active to refrain from sex until marriage. Extend this challenge in love, without any hint of condemnation, stressing what a joy and blessing it is to live according to the truth and meaning of our sexuality. This is not repressive, but truly liberating! For it's by living according to the truth of our sexuality that we "fulfill the very meaning of our being and existence."

Note: The sharing of past hurts or sins is a very delicate matter. The revelation of too many details can, depending on the maturity level of the couple, create additional problems. Instructors should stress the importance of prudence on the couples' part and encourage individuals to address their needs in sacramental confession, through healing prayer and, if necessary, by obtaining professional counseling.

Suggestion: At the end of this talk, encourage all Catholics to go to the Sacrament of Penance as a means of preparing for the worthy celebration of the Sacrament of Marriage. It is likely that most Catholics in the audience haven't been to confession in many years and may have apprehensions about returning. It's important to put them at ease and dispel the common myths surrounding this sacrament. It's also important to stress the healing effects of this sacrament.

union is among the most important things you can do to prepare for the sacrament of marriage.

- Sexual honesty for the engaged means reserving sexual intimacy until it is an honest expression of the wedding vows to which you've already committed your lives before God and his Church.

66-68
70-81

 POINTS TO PONDER

Some people say that once a couple has "crossed the line" and had sex outside marriage, there's no turning back. Is a return to sexual honesty possible? How might such a return affect a couple's marriage?

69-70

- Sexual honesty before you marry also means examining your "past" in light of the true meaning of sex. It means forgiving those who may have wronged you, and it may mean asking forgiveness of your future spouse if you were unfaithful "in advance."

100-102 **DVD**
SEGMENT 6: *4:45*
The Wounds of the Past and the Hope for Healing

Despite excuses we may tend to make, somewhere in our hearts we know we're meant to give ourselves sexually only to one person — our spouse.

- In today's world many people enter marriage with memories and wounds from past sexual experiences. Numerous people can attest that these don't just "go away" when a person gets married. They need to be addressed. Not dwelt upon, but honesty addressed in sacramental Confession, through healing prayer, and, if necessary, by obtaining professional counseling.

- When left unaddressed, men and women with previous sexual experiences often enter marriage with an underlying sense of hurt, suspicion, and mistrust towards each other. Flashbacks and comparisons can actually cripple a couple from experiencing true marital intimacy. But renewed (7) _____virginity_____ is possible if we seek a genuine conversion of our hearts.

69-70
71-74

- Since we're called to love one another as Christ loves, when a future spouse shows genuine sorrow for his or her past sexual choices, (8) _____forgiveness_____ is the only proper response.

This is different from saying it's "OK." Forgiveness acknowledges that an offense was committed, but relinquishes any "right" to harbor resentment or hold that sin over the person's head.

- Furthermore, although this is often even more difficult, forgiving (9) _____yourself_____ for past sexual choices is just as important as forgiving your future spouse.

POINTS TO PONDER

Peter probably considered himself generous when he approached Jesus and asked, "Lord, how often shall my brother sin against me and I forgive him? As many as seven times? Jesus responded, "Seventy times seven [times]" (Mt 18:21-22). Jesus extends forgiveness to us without limit when we express genuine sorrow and repentance. We're called to do the same. We see here, once again, the need to open our hearts to Christ's love. It's impossible on our own to extend such unbounded forgiveness to those who have hurt us. But when offenses have been committed, what's the alternative to genuine repentance and the granting of forgiveness?

Summary
What's It Mean for Our Marriage?

- Mature sexual love is attracted not only by qualities of a person that can always be found in someone else and often to a higher degree. Mature sexual love is attracted to the mystery of the person which is absolutely unrepeatable.

- Sexual honesty means speaking the "language of the body" truthfully. It means learning to love as God loves — freely, totally, faithfully, and fruitfully — with our bodies. Above all, it means never using someone as a means of selfish pleasure.

- Since sexual intercourse is meant to renew and express wedding vows, sexual honesty for engaged couples means reserving sexual intimacy until after the marriage bond has been established. It also means re-examining attitudes and behaviors that have kept you from a true understanding of sexual union and its marital meaning.

Private Reflection Exercise

Sex is meant to express God's free, faithful, eternal, life-giving love. That is, it's meant to express wedding vows. This is the unconditional love that our hearts desire. This is the unconditional love that our hearts (and bodies) deserve. This is the joy and challenge of sexual honesty.

Our culture continually bombards us with a very different message. Sadly, what our society calls "love" is often not love at all, but use of another person. We are never meant to use or be used for the sake of sexual gratification (not even within marriage...), only to love and be loved — as God loves — in total, mutual self-giving.

People today have been deeply affected by society's constant message. We've not been given the tools to understand and embrace the true meaning of sex. Consequently, many enter marriage with "regrets" from the past. But there is always hope to be found in God's mercy and forgiveness. He can heal the wounds in our hearts from wrong sexual choices, if we allow him to (for Catholics, the Sacrament of Penance is a great place to start...).

Whenever people engage in sex that is not an expression of marriage, it actually injures their ability to enjoy true sexual expression when they do marry. Therefore, it is very important to address our pasts in a spirit of repentance and forgiveness, in order to ensure a happy future.

1. How has my family and society influenced the way I understand sex? Do I agree that sex is meant to express the divine love of wedding vows? If not, what is sex meant to express?

2. *If I've had previous sexual relationships, how have they affected the way I relate now to my fiancé(e)? Have I ever asked forgiveness from my future spouse for not saving myself for him/her? If not, am I willing to do so? How might this affect our relationship?*

3.   *If I'm sexually active with my fiancé(e) now, am I willing to wait until our sexual expression can be an honest renewal of our wedding vows? If not, why not? What can we do in addition to saving sex for marriage that will help us understand sexual union as an expression and renewal of our wedding vows?*

How healthy do you think a marriage would be in which the spouses regularly renewed their vows to one another, and everytime they did so, strengthened their commitment to them?

GN, p. 87

NOTE: Like Christ's teaching on the Eucharist in John 6, the Church's teaching on marital chastity — most specifically, contraception — is a "point of departure" for many. You can expect resistance from some participants. So, as St. Peter said, "...be prepared to make a defense to anyone who calls you to account for the hope that is in you, yet do it with gentleness and reverence" (1 Pt 3:15, emphasis added).

In that vain, you are strongly encouraged to familiarize yourself thoroughly with chapters 5, 6, and 7 of *Good News...* before giving this talk. Many of the objections addressed there were actually raised by engaged couples in the development of this course.

Purpose of this talk:

- to help couples understand what it means to be sexually honest within marriage, emphasizing the joy such honesty brings without minimizing the challenge it involves;

- to explain clearly and convincingly the soundness of the Church's teaching against contraception;

- to explain clearly and convincingly the crucial moral distinction between contraception and natural family planning;

- to hold out Christ's gift of grace which truly empowers us, despite our weaknesses, to live the truth.

Logistics: This talk should last approximately 45 minutes.

Suggestion: You may wish to begin this talk by posing the questions at the beginning of chapter 5 of *Good News...* (see pages 87-88), or see video.

Note: Careful study of the video is essential here in order to make the most out of this exercise. Of course you are encouraged, as always, to integrate your own examples and ideas as well.

| The Joy of Sexual Honesty Within Marriage | 87-148 |

1. Remaining Faithful to Your Wedding Vows

87-88

DVD ◉
SEGMENT 1: *8:15*
Being Faithful to
Your Wedding Vows

An unshakable, internal commitment to live out your marriage vows faithfully — no matter what the cost, no matter what the sacrifice — is the (1) _____first_____ ingredient required for a successful marriage.

 POINTS TO PONDER

How healthy would a marriage be if a couple were continually unfaithful to their wedding vows? On the other hand, how healthy would a marriage be if a couple regularly renewed their wedding vows, and every time they did were more committed to them that day than they were the day before?

Simply getting married doesn't automatically guarantee sexual honesty. For example, if spouses are just going through the motions and don't *mean* what they're saying — or worse, if they're in some way trying to *cancel* what their union means — then they are being sexually dishonest.

68

89

1a. The spouses' effort to make their sexual union a faithful expression of their marriage commitment presents "the internal problem of every marriage" (LR, 225).

All questions of sexual morality come down to one basic question.

• Is this an authentic sign of God's free, total, faithful, fruitful love or is it not?

• In other words, is this a faithful expression of wedding vows or is it not?

Let's look at each of the elements of the marriage commitment separately to see what the challenge of sexual honesty really involves. Don't be afraid to embrace it! Accepting the challenge of true love brings true joy — the joy for which you most deeply long.

90-91

Suggestion: Contrast society's notion of sexual freedom understood as sexual license (i.e., never having to say no to your passions) with true sexual freedom understood as the ability to say "yes" to the truth of sex and "no" to distortions of it. If a person can't say "no," is he truly free? Or, rather, is he bound by chains to his passions? Note the twisting of words and their meaning. What society promotes as sexual "freedom" is nothing other than the promotion of sexual slavery.

Note: On this latter point (climax apart from intercourse) it's important to distinguish between male and female climax (see *Good News...* pp. 90-91)

Note: Because this final point is so contested, the remainder of this talk will be devoted to explaining the Church's teaching against contraception and the essential difference of practicing periodic abstinence with NFP.

Free: manipulations, coerced sex, sex only as a response to uncontrollable passions, etc.

DVD
SEGMENT 2: *6:45*
Freedom of the
Sexual Relationship
in Marriage

Total: emotional distance or barriers, refusal to be vulnerable, climax apart from intercourse, etc.

Faithful: fantasizing about someone else during sex (or any other time), etc.

DVD
SEGMENT 3: *7:00*
Fidelity in Marriage

Open to Children: any and every method of contraception

DVD
SEGMENT 4: *2:45*
Fruitfulness in Marriage

 POINTS TO PONDER

Are you looking for a way out of the logic that you must remain open to children for sex to be a true act of love and renewal of your wedding vows? You have a few choices. See *Good News About Sex & Marriage,* question 1, p. 109.

2. Not Just a "Catholic Issue"

121-128

DVD
SEGMENT 5: *5:30*
The Contraception Quiz

Who said the following? Your choices are Gandhi, Sigmund Freud, John Paul II, Theodore Roosevelt, Dr. Ruth, and T.S. Eliot.

- Contraception is "the one sin for which the penalty is national death, race death; a sin for which there is no atonement."

(2) _____Theodore Roosevelt_____

- The sexual urge is "a vector of aspiration along which [our] whole existence develops and perfects itself from within."

(3) _____John Paul II_____

- "The abandonment of the reproductive function is the common feature of all sexual perversions. We actually describe a sexual activity as perverse if it has given up the aim of reproduction and pursues the attainment of pleasure as an aim independent of it."

(4) _____Sigmund Freud_____

- Contraceptive methods are "like putting a premium on vice. They make men and women reckless. Nature is relentless and will have full revenge for any such violation of her laws.... If [contraceptive] methods become the order of the day, nothing but moral degradation can be the result. As it is, man has sufficiently degraded woman for his lust, and [contraception], no matter how well meaning the advocates may be, will still further degrade her."

(5) _____Gandhi_____

Suggestion: Scales often fall off of people's eyes when the interior "logic" of contraception and its damaging effects on society are demonstrated. An overview of contraception's role in the breakdown of society can be found on pages 121-124 of *Good News*.... See the video for an example of how to present this.

Suggestion: For the sake of clarity in discussing the issue, you are strongly encouraged to drop the word "artificial" from the discussion altogether and simply use the word "contraception" when referring to what the Church opposes. The phrase "artificial contraception" is the most misleading and confusing of all since it implies that NFP is in some way "natural contraception." NFP is not contraception at all. This is the precise difference. Preciseness in language is very important to help couples understand the soundness of the Church's teaching.

- By accepting contraception, "the world is trying ...to form a civilized but non-Christian, mentality. The experiment will fail; but we must be very patient in waiting its collapse; meanwhile redeeming the time so that the Faith may be preserved alive through the dark ages before us; to renew and rebuild civilization and save the world from suicide."

(6) _____ T.S. Eliot _____

Every Christian Church was unanimous in its condemnation of contraception as harmful to marriage and society until (7) _____ 1930 _____. At that time the Anglican Church broke with this teaching and accepted contraception within marriage.

Catholics, Protestants, and secular writers alike predicted that societies which embraced contraception would experience an increase in adultery, divorce, premarital sex, out-of-wedlock births, abortion, "fatherless" children, poverty, violence, homosexual activity, etc.

DVD⊙
SEGMENT 6: *5:00*
Consequences of
Contraception

 POINTS TO PONDER

The societal chaos predicted to follow from the acceptance of contraception is upon us. Is the Catholic Church really "out of touch" for maintaining the immorality of contraception, or has society perhaps lost touch with the real meaning of sexuality and its far reaching consequences?

43

121-124

3. The Contradiction of Contraception

107-115 **DVD⊙**
SEGMENT 7: *12:00*
Contraception and
Your Marriage Vows

To contradict means to "speak *against*." Contra-ception is a *contra-diction* of the very language of marital love. It turns the "I do" of wedding vows into an "I do ...*not*." 109-112

3a. The language of the body has "clear-cut meanings" all of which are "'programmed' ...in the conjugal consent." For example, to "the question: 'Are you willing to accept responsibly and with love the children that God may give you...?" — the man and the woman reply: 'Yes'" (TB, 363, 364).

Not only does contraception speak against the commitment to remain open to children. A closer look reveals that it contradicts each of the elements of the marriage commitment.

- *Free:* It is assumed that contraception was invented to prevent pregnancy. However, we already had a 100% safe, 100% reliable way of doing that.

- *Total:* Contracepted intercourse says, "I give myself to you totally... *no I don't.*"

- *Faithful:* How can we speak of fidelity when we're violating freedom, total self-giving, and openness to children?

 POINTS TO PONDER

We take pills, have surgeries, and use technological devices to help maladies and cure disease. That's a good use of medicine and technology. Is fertility a disease?

115-116

4. Responsible Parenthood

112-119

It's a myth that the Church teaches couples are obligated to have as many children as is physically possible. The Church calls couples to a *responsible* exercise of parenthood.

4a. Those "are considered 'to exercise responsible parenthood who prudently and generously decide to have a large family, or who, for serious reasons and with due respect to the moral law, choose to have no more children for the time being or even for an indeterminate period'" (TB, 394).

So, what could a couple do if they had a "serious reason" to avoid a child that wouldn't violate the meaning of intercourse as a sign of God's love?

- Abstaining from intercourse is in no way contraceptive.

- Contraception is the choice to engage in an act of intercourse but *render* it sterile.

- In order to render an act of intercourse sterile (in order to contracept), you must first engage in the act.

- Abstinence is the choice not to "speak" rather than to "speak-*against.*"

Another question arises. Would a couple be doing anything to violate their wedding vows if they had intercourse on a day on which they knew they were naturally infertile?

Note: There will most certainly be doubts as to whether or not there is any substantial difference between contraception and NFP. The approach taken in the videos has been tested and refined over ten years with tens of thousands of audience members. Without a doubt, of all the attempts this author (Christopher West) has made to explain the moral distinction between contraception and NFP, the approach in the videos has proven most effective. However, the logic has to be presented step by step for it to succeed. In the course of the presentation it is important to be aware of the general disposition couples have toward children. Those with an "anti-child" mentality will have the greatest difficulty seeing any distinction between NFP and contraception.

Note: The purpose of this portion of the talk is to remind couples that living the Church's teaching is not a matter of "pulling themselves up by their own bootstraps" but of relying on God's grace, through faith, to empower them to love rightly. Rejection of the Church's teaching on contraception ultimately points to a lack of faith in Christ's gift of redemption. We must always recall that the main task of Catholic marriage preparation is to witness to Christ and invite couples into deeper relationship with one another through a deeper relationship with Christ.

- Herein lies the principle of Natural Family Planning (NFP).

- NFP is acceptable not because it's "natural" as opposed to "artificial," but because it is in keeping with the nature of sexual intercourse as a renewal of the couple's wedding vows.

- Never does a couple using NFP do anything to sterilize their acts of intercourse. If pregnancy does not result from their acts of intercourse, it's God's doing, not their doing. Every time such a couple have intercourse they can honestly pray, "Lord, your will be done."

4b. The difference between contraception and periodic abstinence "is much wider and deeper than is usually thought, one which involves in the final analysis two irreconcilable concepts of the human person and of human sexuality" (FC, n. 32).

 POINTS TO PONDER
Since Christ said it was possible to commit adultery "in the heart" without actually having sex with someone else, wouldn't limiting sex to the infertile time be akin to committing contraception "in the heart"?

118-120

5. A Question of Faith

Many object that the Church's teaching doesn't correspond to our real possibilities.

- Christ reveals another vision of our possibilities.

- We must be careful not to fall into the trap of "holding the form of religion" while "denying the power of it" (2 Tim 3:5).

- For the Church, it's a question of faith. The Church fully believes that Christ can empower us to love as he loves.

5a. What "are the 'concrete possibilities of man'? And of which man are we speaking? Of man dominated by lust or of man redeemed by Christ? This is what is at stake: the reality of Christ's redemption. Christ has redeemed us! This means He has given us the possibility of realizing the entire truth of our being; He has set our freedom free from the domination of [lust]. And if redeemed man still sins, this is not due to an imperfection of Christ's redemptive act, but to man's will not to avail himself of the grace which flows from that act. God's command is of course proportioned to man's capabilities; but to the capabilities of the man to whom the Holy Spirit has been given" (VS, n. 103).

Summary

What's It Mean for Our Marriage?

- Simply getting married doesn't guarantee sexual honesty. Couples need to foster in their minds and hearts an understanding of marital intercourse as an expression and renewal of the commitments they made at the altar. This presents the internal challenge of every marriage.

- When lived honestly, sexual union serves continually to strengthen and deepen a couples marriage bond. However, when couples don't mean what they are saying — or worse, if they're in some way trying to cancel what their union means — sexual intercourse serves subtly to undermine and weaken the intimate friendship of spouses.

- The Church calls couples to a responsible exercise of parenthood. Responsible parenthood contradicts both the mentality that children are a burden to be avoided and the idea that couples should have as many children as is physically possible. Responsible parenthood also involves an unwavering respect for the divine language of love inscribed in the sexual union.

Purpose of this talk:

- to provide key points of overview about NFP — how it works, its effectiveness, etc.;
- to dispel some common myths and misunderstandings about NFP;
- to demonstrate the practical benefits of NFP;
- to encourage couples to take a full course of NFP instruction;
- to encourage couples to practice NFP in their marriages when and if they have serious reason to avoid a child.

Logistics: This talk should last approximately 30 minutes.

Note: The abortifacient nature of these contraceptives will surprise most people. It is important not to undermine the seriousness of the matter. Some canon lawyers have indicated that couples who enter marriage taking contraceptives that they know can cause abortions act in a way so opposed to the "good of children" that their marriage could be invalid from the start.

Some Practical Benefits of Natural Family Planning

128-131

- Modern methods of NFP are safe and have been clinically proven to be 98-99% effective at avoiding pregnancy when used properly.

- Modern methods of NFP are not to be confused with the older "rhythm method." This method was less effective because it depended upon the regularity of a woman's cycle.

- Modern methods of NFP are based on the readily observable signs of fertility present in each cycle (primarily cervical mucus, but also temperature, changes in the cervix, and other signs). So any woman regardless of the regularity or irregularity of her cycles can use NFP effectively.

- NFP is in *no way contraceptive.* It does not work *against* God's creative design for sexual intercourse, but works in complete accord with it.

- NFP is also very effective at helping couples achieve pregnancy when desired.

- NFP has no harmful side effects. (Not only do some contraceptives pose serious health risks, but the pill, Depo-Provera, Norplant, and the IUD can also act as *abortifacients* by preventing a newly → conceived child from implanting in his or her mother's uterus.)

- NFP fosters authentic marital love, respect, honesty, and communication.

- NFP fosters trust in God, not only in a couple's sexual relationship, but in all areas of life.

- NFP promotes an authentic marital spirituality and deepens the couple's relationship with Christ and his Church.

- NFP is marriage insurance. Surveys indicate that couples who practice NFP have a practically non-existent divorce rate. Why? Mainly because practicing NFP fosters those very same virtues that are necessary for a healthy marriage. It allows intercourse to be a true expression, renewal, and deepening of the couple's commitment to marriage.

DVD
SEGMENT 1: *5:15*
What is Natural
Family Planning?

DVD
SEGMENT 2: *3:30*
Natural Family Planning
is Not Contraceptive

115

DVD
SEGMENT 3: *8:15*
The Benefits of
Natural Family Planning

144-145

116

I-50

Suggestion: End the talk with a final word of encouragement to take a full course of instruction in NFP if they haven't done so already. You might help them recognize that if they expect to have reason to space their children or limit their family size that it simply doesn't make sense to choose a method for doing so without having all the facts. Taking an NFP class is the only way to get the full picture.

Let's take a look at the marriage commitments again, this time through
the lens of NFP.

DVD
SEGMENT 4: *3:30*
Your Marriage Vows
through the Lens of
Natural Family Planning

Free: Practicing NFP puts a couple's freedom to the test. The ability to say "no"
is essential to the ability to say "yes" authentically. Thus, NFP fosters true
freedom in marriage.

Total: NFP fosters respect for the total person and respect for the meaning of
total self-giving. Refusal to erect chemical or physical barriers enables
spouses to let go of the emotional barriers too.

Faithful: Fidelity to the marriage vows is the raison d'etre of NFP.

Open to Children: This is the hallmark of NFP.

DVD
SEGMENT 5: *5:30*
The Wedding
Invitation Analogy

POINTS TO PONDER

Very few doctors are educated about modern, scientific methods of NFP,
but virtually all are well versed in contraception. Why do you think that's
the case?

Logistics: Repeat the same procedure from the previous private reflections.

Private Reflection Exercise

1. Look ahead to your married life and assume at some point that you have a just reason to avoid a pregnancy. Are you afraid of the abstinence from sex that NFP would require? If so, why? If not, is there anything else that threatens you about the idea of practicing NFP? If so, what?

Bride and groom promise at the altar to "receive children lovingly from God." Children are, in fact, the supreme gift and fulfillment of married love. Still, many couples in today's world encounter times in their married life when they find it necessary, with just reason, to avoid a pregnancy. When NFP is properly presented and typical misconceptions are clarified, it seems there are still two main reasons people resist the idea of practicing it: (1) fear of abstinence and (2) fear of relinquishing a sense of "control" over one's fertility.

2. Does the thought of this make you uneasy? If so, why? If not, is there anything else that threatens you about the idea of practicing NFP? If so, what?

NFP, when properly taught and practiced, is actually more effective at avoiding pregnancy than most every contraceptive on the market. It is self-evident that you simply can't get pregnant if you don't have sex when you're fertile. Still, couples intuit that practicing NFP involves trusting God with their lives and their fertility. When they choose to have intercourse, they must relinquish "control" and allow God to decide whether or not a new life comes into the world from their union.

Answers

God's Plan for Marriage "in the Beginning:" Male & Female He Created Them
1. marriage
2. free, total, faithful, fruitful
3. marriage
4. freedom
5. love
6. love

Christ Restores God's Plan for Marriage: Male & Female He Redeemed Them
1. wedding
2. love
3. redemption
4. serve
5. return
6. sacramental

What Are You Saying "I Do" to?: The Basics of Marriage in the Church
1. flesh
2. prototype
3. bride & groom
4. witness
5. vows
6. bodies
7. consummated

8. flesh
9. renewing
10. impediments
11. form
12. freely and unconditionally
13. fidelity, indissolubility, children

The Joy of Sexual Honesty before Marriage
1. marriage
2. unrepeatable
3. language
4. using
5. Truth and love
6. marital
7. virginity
8. forgiveness
9. yourself

The Joy of Sexual Honesty within Marriage
1. first
2. Theodore Roosevelt[1]
3. John Paul II[2]
4. Sigmund Freud[3]
5. Gandhi[4]
6. T.S. Eliot[5]
7. 1930

1 Cited in Patrick Fagan, "A Culture of Inverted Sexuality," *Catholic World Report,* November 1998, p. 57

2 *Love & Responsibility,* p. 46

3 Introductory Lectures in Psychoanalysis (New York: W.W. Norton and Company, 1966), p. 392

4 Cited in Patrick Fagan, "A Culture of Inverted Sexuality," *Catholic World Report,* November 1998, p. 57

5 *Thoughts after Lambeth* (London: Faber and Faber, 1931), p. 32

Acknowledgments

Ascension Press is pleased to publish *God's Plan for a Joy-Filled Marriage*. We are particularly grateful to the following individuals who have been invaluable in the development of this program. Many thanks to the many priests and lay leaders in Denver, too numerous to mention, who helped in the process of developing these materials. We also thank the thousands of couples over the years who experienced the *God's Plan* program and have shared their verbal and written suggestions for the program's on-going development. Special thanks to Christopher West, Archbishop Charles Chaput, Fran Maier, Steve Weidenkopf, David Walker, Tom McCabe, Matthew Pinto, Ed Mechmann, Sr. Mary Elizabeth Reis, S.V.D., Adriana James, Christopher Mueller, Jake Samour, and Wendy West for their various contributions.

Evaluation Form

Date of Program: _____   Instructor: _____

Your feedback is very important to us. Please honestly evaluate the program and answer the following questions.

Please circle one:

1. *I am*   MALE   FEMALE

Please check one box per question:

		Very Helpful	Helpful	Not Helpful
2.	Overall, I found the program to be:			
3.	I found the instructor to be:			
4.	I found the workbook to be			
5.	I found the reflection exercises to be:			

Please circle one response per question:

6. I now have a better understanding of the Church's teaching about marriage: YES   NO   SOMEWHAT

7. This program has affected my relationship with God: POSITIVELY   NEGATIVELY   INDIFFERENTLY

8. This program has affected my impression of the Catholic Church: POSITIVELY   NEGATIVELY   INDIFFERENTLY

9. On the back of this evaluation, describe what you found most helpful about the program and why. What would you suggest we change? Offer any additional comments (constructive criticisms & compliments are both helpful).

Confidential Survey

The following questions are of a personal nature. There is no obligation to answer them. However, your anonymous responses will help in our on-going efforts to better understand the profile and needs of those coming to the Catholic Church for marriage.

Please circle one response per question:

1. I consider myself a(n):   CATHOLIC   NON-CATHOLIC CHRISTIAN   AGNOSTIC   ATHEIST   OTHER

2. My fiancé(e) is a(n):   CATHOLIC   NON-CATHOLIC CHRISTIAN   AGNOSTIC   ATHEIST   OTHER

3. I attend church: REGULARLY   SOMETIMES   RARELY   NEVER

4. I attended Catholic School: YES   NO

5. (IF YES TO #4) Please circle the following category that best indicates your highest completed level of Catholic schooling:

K – 8TH GRADE   HIGH SCHOOL   COLLEGE

	YES	NO	
6. I plan to be more active in my faith as a result of this class	YES	NO	MAYBE
7. I have made a deeper commitment to Christ as a result of this class:	YES	NO	
8. My fiancé(e) and I are living together:	YES	NO	
9. My fiancé(e) and I have been sexually active:	YES	NO	
10. (IF YES TO #9) We now plan on saving sex until we are married:	YES	NO	NOT SURE
11. We had been planning to use contraception in our marriage:	YES	NO	NOT SURE
12. (IF YES to #11) We still plan on using contraception in our marriage:	YES	NO	NOT SURE
13. We definitely want to practice NFP in our marriage:	YES	NO	NOT SURE

14. I would like to have   1 – 2   3 – 4   5 – 6   more than 6   children in our marriage.